This Notebook Belongs To :

____

Made in the USA
Columbia, SC
16 August 2020

16485604R00061